Inventions and Investigations

Andrew Solway

Raintree

www.raintreepublishers.co.uk
Visit our website to find out
more information about
Raintree books.

To order:
☎ Phone 0845 6044371
📄 Fax +44 (0) 1865 312263
✉ Email myorders@raintreepublishers.co.uk

Customers from outside the UK please telephone +44 1865 312262

Raintree is an imprint of Capstone Global Library
Limited, a company incorporated in England and
Wales having its registered office at 7 Pilgrim Street,
London, EC4V 6LB – Registered company number:
6695582

Text © Capstone Global Library Limited 2010
First published in paperback in 2011

The moral rights of the proprietor have been asserted.

Edited by Sabrina Crewe
Designed by Sabine Beaupré
Original illustrations © Discovery Books Limited 2009
Illustrated by Stefan Chabluk
Picture research by Sabrina Crewe
Originated by Modern Age
Printed by and bound by CTPS (China Translation and
   Printing Services Ltd)

ISBN 978 1 406211 84 9 (hardback)
13 12 11 10 09
10 9 8 7 6 5 4 3 2 1

ISBN 978 1 406211 91 7 (paperback)
14 13 12 11 10
10 9 8 7 6 5 4 3 2 1

British Library Cataloguing in Publication Data
Solway, Andrew.
   Inventions and investigations. -- (Sci-Hi)
   1. Research--Juvenile literature.
   2. Inventions--Juvenile literature.
   3. Discoveries in science--Juvenile literature.
   I. Title II. Series
   570.1-dc22

Acknowledgements
We would like to thank the following for permission
to reproduce photographs: © European Space
Agency/NASA p. **18**; © Getty Images pp. **12** (Michael
Melford), **43**; © MODIS Oceans Group, NASA Goddard
Space Flight Center p. **40**; © NASA pp. **28**, **41** left, **42**;
© NASA/Goddard Space Flight Center p. **4**; © NASA/
Boeing Company p. **41** right; © NOAA p. **22**; © SeaWiFS
Project, NASA/Goddard Space Flight Center, and
ORBIMAG p. **38**; © Shutterstock cover inset (Yellowj),
pp. **3** top (Ron from York), **3** bottom (RCP Photo),
6 (Mark Lorch), **7** (Danny Warren), **8** (Jason Maehl),
9 (Armin Rose), **11** (Serg Zastavkin), **13** all, **14** both,
19 (Stepan Jezek), **21** (Ron from York), **24** (Planner),
26 (Russell Shively), **29** (Lorraine Kourafas), **30** (James
Doss), **31** (Vera Bogaerts), **33** all, **34** (RCP Photo),
37 (Inc), **39** (George Muresan).

Cover photograph of the Icelandic Low, an area
of low atmospheric pressure, reproduced with
permission of NASA.

We would like to thank content consultant Suzy
Gazlay and text consultant Nancy Harris for their
invaluable help in the preparation of this book.

Every effort has been made to contact copyright
holders of material reproduced in this book. Any
omissions will be rectified in subsequent printings if
notice is given to the publishers.

Disclaimer
All the Internet addresses (URLs) given in this book
were valid at the time of going to press. However, due
to the dynamic nature of the Internet, some addresses
may have changed, or sites may have changed or
ceased to exist since publication. While the author and
Publishers regret any inconvenience this may cause
readers, no responsibility for any such changes can be
accepted by either the author or the Publishers.

Contents

What inventions happened by accident? Go to page 8 to find out!

What invention used on the Moon is used by you? See page 43!

Some words are shown in bold, **like this**. These words are explained in the glossary. You will find important information and definitions underlined, <u>like this</u>.

From Ideas to Inventions

How many inventions did you use before breakfast? Maybe your alarm clock woke you up. But did you know that the first accurate clock was invented by Dutch scientist Christiaan Huygens in 1657?

Was the radio on when you came downstairs? A Canadian, Reginald Fessenden, made the first radio broadcast in 1906. And if you had cereal for breakfast, you'll be interested to know that the first ready-to-eat breakfast cereal, called granula, was invented by James Caleb Jackson in the USA in 1863.

Then you probably brushed your teeth. For that, you could thank Englishman William Addis. He made some of the first toothbrushes in 1780.

What is an invention?

So what is an invention? <u>An invention is something new and useful</u>. Some inventions are things, while others are processes, or ways of doing something. These inventions have made our society the way it is today. Some inventions, such as clocks, were invented hundreds of years ago and are still used. Others, such as mobile phones, have changed our world in only a few years.

An inventor is someone who has good ideas for inventions. But an idea is not enough by itself. It has to be tested. This is where investigations come in. <u>Investigations are experiments that try out new ideas</u>. They test scientific **theories** (ideas). With investigations, scientists find out if an invention is practical and useful.

In this book, you will learn about the processes of investigating and inventing. And you'll learn how they affect you!

All-time top invention

What do you think is the most important everyday invention: the car, the microwave, the toothbrush, or the mobile phone? What would life be like without these inventions? A survey in the USA asked children and adults which of these inventions they could not live without. The winner was a surprise: it was the toothbrush!

Testing ideas

Investigations are like scientific experiments. They involve testing an invention under strict conditions. Inventors must ask themselves several questions. Does the original idea work? Is it reliable (does it keep working)? Could the invention be made more simply or cheaply? An invention is not useful if it is too expensive.

Not all investigations are experiments in laboratories. Many hundreds of years ago, scientists such as the famous Galileo would spend hours observing the night skies. They made important discoveries about their own world and beyond.

Try and try again

Inventors sometimes need good luck during their investigations. The US inventor Charles Goodyear wanted to make rubber that would not go soft in hot weather and crack in cold weather. He spent

Patents

A **patent** is a way for inventors to stop other people taking their ideas. If an inventor applies for a patent, the patent office checks that no one else has already registered the same idea. If nobody has, the inventor gets a patent. Anyone who wants to use the new invention must pay the inventor.

Rubber is used for tyres, so we all depend on Goodyear's improved rubber when we travel.

years investigating rubber, a natural material that comes from the sap of a tree. He mixed in different chemicals and tested the **properties** of these mixtures. He tested them for strength and flexibility under different conditions.

Goodyear found the way to make better rubber by accident. He was handling a new mixture one day in 1839 when he accidentally spilt some of it on a stove. When he tested the spilt mixture, Goodyear found that it stayed strong and springy in both hot and cold weather. He had made a weatherproof rubber at last. Goodyear's invention was named vulcanized rubber. Today it is used for everything from rubber bands to waterproof clothing and car tyres.

For more lucky accidents that led to inventions, turn the page!

Accidental Inventions

Many inventors have had lucky accidents that led to **breakthroughs** and new inventions. However, as the French scientist Louis Pasteur said, "Chance favours the prepared mind". He meant that a good inventor notices when something unusual happens and takes advantage of it. Here are a few examples of those kinds of inventions.

Ice-cream cone

Before 1904, ice cream was always served on plates or in bowls. At the 1904 World's Fair in St Louis, Missouri, USA, an ice-cream seller ran out of dishes. A neighbouring waffle seller, Ernest Hamwi, rolled his waffles into cones to serve ice cream in. Edible ice-cream cups had been made before, but this happy accident made ice-cream cones popular.

Pacemaker

Doctors use pacemakers for people with certain heart problems. A pacemaker keeps a heart beating steadily. In the 1950s, the US **engineer** Wilson Greatbatch made a mistake when he was making an electrical **circuit** to measure heartbeats. The circuit pulsed, and then it was quiet for a moment. Greatbatch realized it was like a heartbeat. He had created a pacemaker, which was first used in humans in 1960.

Teflon

In 1938, US chemist Roy Plunkett was looking for a new type of gas to use in fridges. One of the gases he prepared turned into a white powder. Plunkett tested the material and found it was very slippery. He had discovered the non-stick plastic Teflon. Today, many pans we use for cooking are coated with Teflon to stop food from sticking to the pans.

SUPERGLUE

In 1942, US **chemist** Harry Coover was trying to make plastic that people could see through clearly. The chemicals he was working with kept sticking together as soon as they got slightly damp. Later, Coover realized that the chemicals would make a really powerful glue – a superglue!

VELCRO

One day in 1948, Swiss engineer Georges de Mistral went hunting in the Alps. When he got back, he found burrs (prickly seed pods) stuck to his dog and clothes. He looked at the burrs under a microscope and found they were covered in tiny hooks. This gave him the idea for making Velcro. Today we use Velcro for fastening shoes and outdoor clothing as well as many other things.

Lighting Up the World

Electric light at night made life much easier for people in the 19th century.

Let's take a look at how an important invention develops. The story of the electric light bulb shows us just how much work even a simple invention takes.

Imagine what life was like before electric light. Until the 19th century, people used candles, oil lamps, or gas lights. These were not as bright or as convenient as electric light. Electric light bulbs brought bright, clean lighting into homes, offices, and factories.

Bright wire

In 1802, British scientist Humphrey Davy was experimenting with **batteries**. A battery is a device that stores and supplies electricity. In one experiment, Davy put an electric **current,** or stream of electricity, through a thin wire. This made the wire so hot that it glowed brightly.

Adding a bulb

Davy suggested that a glowing wire like this one could be used as a light. But there was a problem with Davy's idea. After only a short time, the **filament**, or hot wire, broke because it reacted with oxygen in the air. In the mid-19th century, the British **chemist** Joseph Swan found an answer to this problem. He put the filament inside a glass bulb. Most of the air was pumped out, so there was little oxygen to cause the filament to break.

Swan's light bulb worked, but he kept investigating. He wanted to improve on his invention, so Swan tried a different pump that got even more air out of the bulb. He also tried using different materials for the filament. Between 1878 and 1880, Swan made a practical bulb that gave a bright light and lasted many hours.

BULB POWER

ONE BICYCLE HEADLAMP CAN GIVE MORE LIGHT THAN 1,000 CANDLES!

Joseph Swan, seen here in his laboratory, kept investigating for many years to improve his light bulb.

Edison's light

Thomas Alva Edison (1847–1931)

Thomas Edison is probably the world's most famous inventor. Light bulbs were not his only inventions. There were more than 1,000 others! They included the first sound recording device, a microphone used in telephones, and an early kind of cinema.

In the USA, inventor Thomas Edison was also experimenting with electric light. In 1878 and 1879, he and a team of researchers tested over 6,000 different materials. They were looking for a good filament. Early in 1880, they found that a filament made from bamboo lasted 1,200 hours without breaking.

Thomas Edison never stopped investigating and inventing, even when he was old.

Later improvements

Several other inventions improved the light bulb over the next 50 years. In 1908 and 1909, William Coolidge of the General Electric Company (GEC) in the USA made a light bulb filament from a metal called tungsten. Tungsten was very tough and could be heated to 2,500°C (4,532°F). It was ideal for light bulb filaments.

In 1913, an US chemist named Irving Langmuir found that filling the bulb with a gas called argon made the bulb twice as bright. Improvements continued. In 1936 and again in 1955, improved filaments made for even better light bulbs.

As you can see from the story of the light bulb, the process of investigation and invention can be a long one. From 1802, when Davy was experimenting with batteries, to 1959 is more than 150 years! And there is still more to come. . .

Matches not needed

When electric lights were first installed, people didn't know how to use them. Most people thought light bulbs needed to be lit with a match!

The first football match under electric lights was played in 1878. It took place in front of a crowd in London.

LIGHTS FOR THE FUTURE

Many discoveries and inventions are made in the research departments of big companies. Two newer kinds of light were developed this way.

Low-energy light

Low-energy light bulbs are more **efficient** than ordinary light bulbs. They use about one-fifth the electricity of a regular bulb.

Low-energy bulbs work in the same way as the long, fluorescent tubes of light you see in schools and offices. These tubes are filled with a gas. A current is put through the gas, causing the tube to fluoresce (glow).

In 1973, US scientist Ed Hammer, who worked for GEC, had an idea. He thought of twisting a fluorescent tube into a spiral. This would make a low-energy bulb small enough to use at home. Hammer produced the first low-energy bulb in 1976. The bulbs are more expensive than regular bulbs, but people are using them to save energy.

LEDs

Back in 1962, another scientist called Nick Holonyak was working at GEC. He invented a new type of light called a light-emitting **diode** (LED). LEDs give off light when an electrical current flows through an electrical device called a diode. The diode controls the flow of the electricity.

Until recently, scientists could only make red, yellow, or blue LEDs. Then, in 2005, a US research student called Michael Bowers made an accidental discovery. Bowers was trying to grow tiny **crystals** (solids that form in regular patterns, like a diamond). His crystals were only one-thousandth the width of a human hair. He found that one batch of the crystals glowed with a soft, white light. Bowers had a bright idea. He tried coating blue LEDs with the crystals and produced a white LED light.

We will soon be seeing more LEDs all around us. They use only one-eighth the energy of an ordinary bulb and last 20 times longer.

More and more people are switching to low-energy light bulbs to save energy.

This **LED** display is at a hospital in Rogers, Arkansas, in the USA. It allows visitors to "paint" with light.

World's biggest LED

LEDs can be used to make large visual display screens. Probably the biggest in the world is in Beijing, China. The screen has 2,292 large LEDs. It covers an area of 2,200 square metres (23,680 square feet).

PRODUCING POWER

It often happens that one invention or new idea leads to others. Light bulbs need electrical power, and their invention led to new ways of producing power. This was really important, because it meant electricity became available for many other uses.

From batteries to generators

At the time that lights were invented, the main way of producing electricity was from **batteries**. However, batteries are expensive to make, and they regularly need recharging.

Scientists did know another way to make electricity. In 1831, Michael Faraday discovered that if he moved a wire close to a strong magnet, it produced a small electric **current**. From this idea, **engineers** developed electric **generators**. A generator is a machine that makes, or generates, electrical energy from other kinds of energy. Energy from steam or water, for example, can turn wire inside a generator fitted with magnets. The movement is turned into an electric current.

Another of Nikola Tesla's inventions was the "Tesla coil". He used it in an attempt to send electricity through the air. This idea failed, but he produced spectacular lightning bolts.

DC or AC?

After developing light bulbs, Thomas Edison decided to create a way to power them. He designed a system for generating electricity on a large scale. In 1882, Edison built an electrical power station at Pearl Street in New York City, USA. Six "Jumbo" **dynamos** each produced enough electricity to power 1,200 light bulbs.

A dynamo is a type of generator that produces direct-current (DC) electricity. This is electricity that flows in one direction. But engineers found that they could not send DC electricity over long distances. A US inventor called Nikola Tesla invented a different kind of generator between 1883 and 1888. This produced alternating-current (AC) electricity. AC electricity constantly changes direction. Tesla's generator had a big advantage. AC could be sent long distances.

Inventing the microwave oven

During World War II, Percy Spencer was chief engineer with the US company Raytheon. Raytheon made **radar** equipment, which used **radio waves** to detect enemy planes and ships. The radio waves used in radar are called microwaves.

The microwaves were produced by a device called a magnetron tube. Spencer noticed that the magnetron tubes gave off heat. One time, a magnetron melted a chocolate bar in his pocket. This gave Spencer the idea for the microwave oven, which he invented in 1946. It was 20 years before microwave ovens were small and cheap enough to use in the home.

Electricity in the home

Electricity can be used to produce several kinds of energy as well as light. It can be turned into movement, heat, and sound.

The invention of **mains electricity**, or electricity supplied from a power station, was very important. Once people had electricity in their homes and businesses, inventors soon found other ways to use it. The electrical inventions of the late 19th and early 20th centuries changed people's lives. New machines made it easier and quicker to do many tasks.

Electric motors

Probably the most useful electrical invention was the electric motor. A motor is basically an electric generator run in reverse. It uses electricity to produce a turning motion.

Belgian engineer Zénobe Gramme made an electric motor by mistake in 1873. That year he was showing two dynamos at an exhibition in Vienna, Austria. He made a mistake when connecting the dynamos together, and one dynamo fed electricity into the other. The second dynamo began to work as a motor. The electric motor gave people a new way of using electricity. They could use it to make things move.

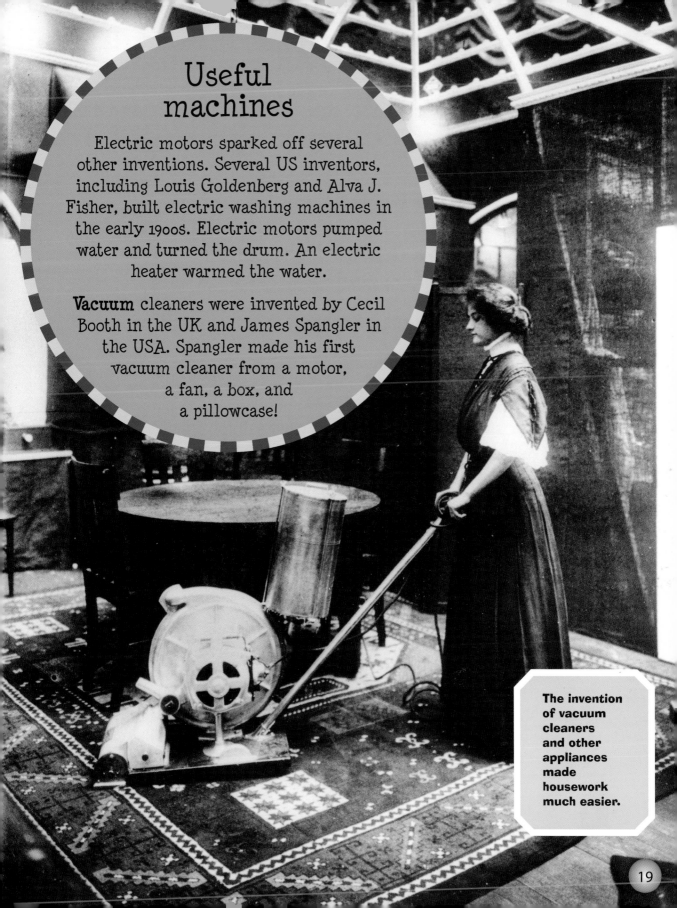

Useful machines

Electric motors sparked off several other inventions. Several US inventors, including Louis Goldenberg and Alva J. Fisher, built electric washing machines in the early 1900s. Electric motors pumped water and turned the drum. An electric heater warmed the water.

Vacuum cleaners were invented by Cecil Booth in the UK and James Spangler in the USA. Spangler made his first vacuum cleaner from a motor, a fan, a box, and a pillowcase!

The invention of vacuum cleaners and other appliances made housework much easier.

SHRINKING ELECTRONICS

Think how many **electronic** devices you use. Computers, phones, and music players are just a few examples. So how were these devices invented? It all started with a failed experiment with a light bulb.

A failed experiment

A problem with early light bulbs was that they gradually turned black with use. At Thomas Edison's laboratory in Menlo Park, New Jersey, USA, researchers tried to solve this problem. In 1883, they put an extra wire, or **electrode**, inside the bulb. Unfortunately this experiment did not work. But the extra electrode did appear to work as a **valve**, which is a device that controls flow. This valve could control the flow of electric **current**. It allowed the current to go in one direction but not the other.

A young British scientist called John Fleming played an important part in this investigation. Later, Fleming went back to the UK to work for Guglielmo Marconi. Marconi was building radios.

Inventing the vacuum tube

Fleming had an idea that the Edison bulb with the extra electrode might be useful in radios. He made a bulb and began to experiment with it. He discovered that it was very good at picking up faint **radio waves** (waves of energy used for communication). The new device, invented in 1904, was called a **vacuum** tube.

Scientists see the invention of the vacuum tube as the birth of electronics. Electronics is the science behind televisions, computers, and other electrical devices that we use.

Diodes and triodes

Fleming's vacuum tube was called a **diode** because it had two electrodes. "Di-" means two. In 1906, a US inventor called Lee De Forest invented another vacuum tube, called a triode, which had three electrodes. "Tri-" means three. The triode worked as an **amplifier**. An amplifier is a device that makes radio signals stronger, or amplifies them. Triodes could amplify the faint radio signals picked up by diodes. Diodes and triodes greatly improved radios of the time. Over the next 40 years, they were also used to build music players, televisions, and other electronic devices.

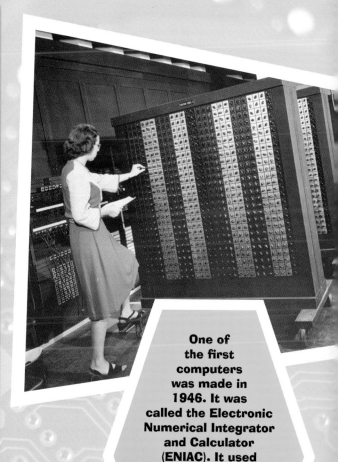

One of the first computers was made in 1946. It was called the Electronic Numerical Integrator and Calculator (ENIAC). It used more than 17,000 vacuum tubes, weighed 27 tonnes (30 tons), and took up a whole room!

Lee De Forest holds his invention, the triode. It was the first vacuum tube that could detect and amplify radio signals.

Investigating semiconductors

<u>Semiconductors are substances that can be treated to control the flow of electricity</u>. Silicon, a substance made from sand, is a semiconductor.

During World War II, scientists found ways of treating semiconductors so that they acted like diodes. After 1945, when the war ended, they began to wonder if semiconductors could replace vacuum tubes in radios and other electronic equipment. Many researchers started investigating semiconductors.

The first transistor

At Bell Laboratories in Murray Hill, New Jersey, in the USA, scientists Walter Brattain, John Bardeen, and William Shockley were all researching semiconductors. In 1947, Brattain and Bardeen made a semiconductor device that amplified a signal, making it 100 times stronger. It was the first transistor. Transistors are semiconductors that work either as amplifiers or switches to control current.

Look at the difference in the size of a vacuum tube (left) and the size of a transistor (right). The small size of transistors made new devices possible.

Getting smaller and more efficient

William Shockley soon improved on the first transistor. His design used two different kinds of semiconductor. The new transistors were much smaller than vacuum tubes. They used less electricity, so they were more **efficient**. By the late 1950s, transistors were being used in all kinds of electronic equipment.

The invention of transistors led to small, portable radios. Young people had access to personal radios for the first time! The new radios had a big impact on music. Radio stations began playing pop music and rock and roll for their new audience.

Accidental amplifier

Walter Brattain made the first transistor almost by accident. The device he was experimenting with was not working because of air bubbles on the outside. As a quick fix for the problem, Brattain put the device in water. To his surprise, he found it worked as an amplifier.

Turn the page to find out how electronics got REALLY small!

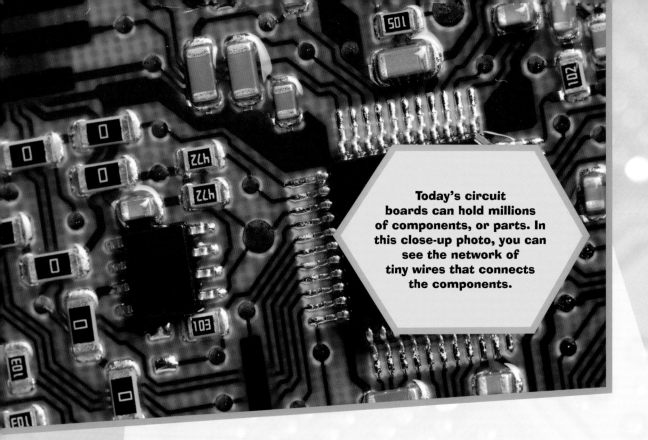

Today's circuit boards can hold millions of components, or parts. In this close-up photo, you can see the network of tiny wires that connects the components.

Transistor troubles

Transistors were small, but not small enough. **Engineers** wanted even smaller parts for complex devices, such as computers and aeroplane controls. But when transistors got very small, it was difficult to connect them together. Technicians had to use microscopes to attach tiny wires. If a speck of dust got in a transistor, the device wouldn't work.

Silicon chips

In the late 1950s, two US scientists came up with an alternative to transistors at almost the same time. They were Jack Kilby at Texas Instruments and Robert Noyce at Fairchild Semiconductor. Instead of making single transistors, Kilby and Noyce put lots of diodes and transistors on a single piece of silicon.

The parts formed a tiny electrical **circuit**. A circuit is an arrangement of parts through which a current can flow.

Kilby and Noyce had invented the **microchip**. Microchips first went on sale in 1961. Since then, the individual parts on a microchip have got smaller and smaller. Kilby's first chip had only one transistor and a few other components. By 2008, computer microchips could hold 2 billion transistors!

Microchips in your pocket

If it wasn't for microchips, there wouldn't be any electronics small enough to put in your pocket. Microchips also make it possible for you to program your computer and use remote controls.

Nanotubes

Carbon **nanotubes** are extremely tiny tubes made from carbon. In 2007, researchers at the Lawrence Berkeley National Laboratory in the USA made a radio from nanotubes. The radio is so small that it could be inserted into a human **cell**! This image shows a magnified nanotube that, at its true size, is 10,000 times thinner than a human hair! The researchers added radio wave lines to the image to show how the nanotube emits a signal.

THE INTERNET

In the last twenty years or so, the Internet has had a huge impact on our world. It has changed how we learn, how we do business, and what we do for fun. What were the important inventions that made the Internet possible? And who came up with them?

First network

In 1969 the very first part of the Internet was put together. It had just three computers! It was called ARPANET, which stands for Advanced Research Projects Agency Network. ARPANET was set up by the US Defense Department.

First email

In 1971 Ray Tomlinson, who worked on ARPANET, developed the first Internet email program. He sent the first email message from one computer to another one right next to it.

The very first email was sent went between the two machines shown here. The only connection between them was through ARPANET.

First Internet game

British computer programmer Roy Trubshaw wrote a version of the game "Dungeons and Dragons" for the Internet in the mid-1970s.

Today, we use the World Wide Web to access much of our information.

The World Wide Web

Until the 1990s, the Internet could only be used by people who knew about computer programming. But in 1990, British computer scientist Tim Berners-Lee invented the World Wide Web. It was made available to the public in 1992. This was the system of websites and web pages that we use today.

Personal computers

In 1981 IBM began selling personal computers. Before this time, the Internet only connected together large computers in universities and other research centres. Now computer scientists began working to connect personal computers to a network.

First Internet radio

Radio HK, the first full-time, Internet-only radio station, started broadcasting in 1995.

Internet use explodes

In 1990 there were about 300,000 computers connected to the Internet world wide. By 1995 there were 16 million users. In 2005 the number of Internet users was 1 billion. By 2008 the number was almost 1.5 billion.

Steam Engines to Biofuels

New discoveries in science can lead to new inventions. A new invention can also lead to new scientific ideas. In this chapter, we will look at how science and inventions are linked in the development of engines.

Steam engines

The first engines ran on the power of steam. British **engineer** Thomas Newcomen came up with the first practical engine in 1712. He took ideas from two earlier engines. One was a design made by French scientist Denis Papin in 1690. It was probably never built. The other was a steam pump made by the English inventor Thomas Savery in 1699. This did not work very well. Newcomen took the best ideas from both engines and combined them to make a much better design.

James Watt (1736–1819)

In the 1760s, Scotsman James Watt became interested in steam engines. He discovered that the Newcomen engine was very **inefficient**. About 80 per cent of the heat put in was wasted. In 1763 to 1764, Watt made many improvements to Newcomen's design. Watt's improvements were so successful that many people believe it was he, not Newcomen, who invented the steam engine.

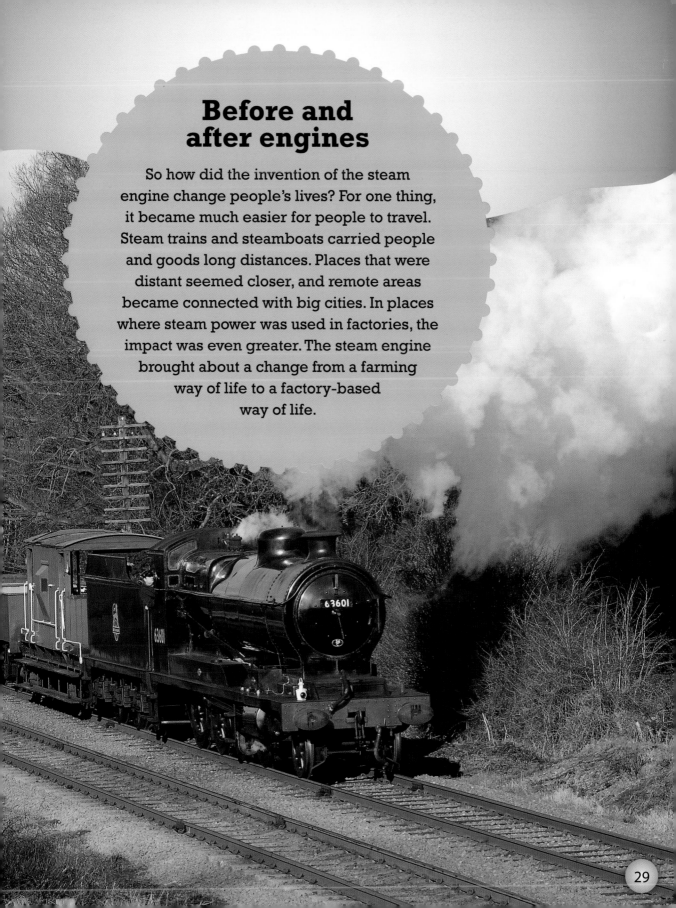

Before and after engines

So how did the invention of the steam engine change people's lives? For one thing, it became much easier for people to travel. Steam trains and steamboats carried people and goods long distances. Places that were distant seemed closer, and remote areas became connected with big cities. In places where steam power was used in factories, the impact was even greater. The steam engine brought about a change from a farming way of life to a factory-based way of life.

Internal combustion

Another engine milestone was achieved in the 1870s. In the internal combustion engine, fuel is combusted, or burned, inside the engine. The first successful internal combustion engines appeared in 1876. The fuel they used was petrol. The petrol is mixed with air and then ignited by a spark plug. The spark plug is the part that creates a spark to start the fuel burning.

Internal combustion engines were lighter and more **efficient** than steam engines. With this new engine, inventors made the first cars. By the 1900s, inventors were using petrol engines in the first aeroplanes.

Diesel engines

In the 1820s, a French scientist called Sadi Carnot had an important idea. He showed that the power we get from an engine depends on the difference in temperature between the hottest part of an engine and the coolest part. Around 1880, a German engineer called Rudolf Diesel used Carnot's ideas in a new type of engine. In the diesel engine, air was squashed until it became very hot. Then fuel was added, and it exploded without needing a spark plug. Modern diesel engines use less fuel than petrol engines. They are used to power lorries, ships, and other machines as well as some cars.

Problems with the environment

Diesel and petrol both come from petroleum. When petrol and diesel engines burn fuel, they release carbon dioxide gas and pollutants into the air. Today's engineers and inventors are finding ways to reduce the amount of **emissions** that engines produce. They are building engines that use less fuel. They are making cleaner types of fuel, too. Biofuels are one kind of clean fuel. They are usually made from plant materials such as sugar-cane or corn oil. Biofuels can also be made from some kinds of **bacteria** (tiny, single-**celled** life forms).

Electric engines

Do you remember Nikola Tesla from page 17, the inventor of the AC **generator**? Tesla Motors is named after him, and it makes electric cars. The Tesla Roadster is an electric-powered sports car. It can go from 0 to 100 kilometres per hour (0 to 60 miles per hour) in about 4 seconds, but it produces no carbon emissions. The **batteries** it runs on are like giant versions of the batteries in laptops and mobile phones. The Tesla can travel around 350 kilometres (220 miles) without a recharge. However, it takes at least 2 hours to "fill up" with electricity.

Making New Materials

We use plastics for everything from toothbrushes to spaceships. But 100 years ago, none of these plastics had been invented.

The **chemists** who developed plastics were inventors. Inventors such as Thomas Edison and James Watt used investigations to invent useful new machines and other devices. Chemical inventors use investigations when they invent new materials.

Polymer chains

All materials are made from tiny **particles** called atoms. Most materials are made from small groups of atoms joined together. These are called **molecules**. Plastics are made from much bigger molecules, called **polymers**. A polymer molecule is a long chain, made up of many smaller molecules joined together.

Many new plastics were invented in the first half of the 20th century. Wallace Carothers was a chemist at DuPont, a chemical company where he invented plastics.

In the early 1920s, a few plastics already existed. However, no one really understood the nature of plastics and polymers. Then a German scientist called Hermann Staudinger began to investigate natural materials, such as rubber and starch. His investigations showed that these materials were polymers too.

An American chemist called Wallace Carothers became interested in Staudinger's ideas. In the 1930s, Carothers worked for the chemical company DuPont. Instead of looking at natural materials, Carothers and his research team tried to make their own polymers. They found a way to join together small molecules in long chains. By using different combinations, they came up with all kinds of new plastics.

You can find out about some of the plastics Carothers made on the following pages!

Make your own plastic

This experiment involves two techniques often used in chemistry:

- Heating makes a reaction happen faster.
- Filtering separates a solid from a liquid.

1. Warm 1 litre (about 2 pints) of milk in a saucepan until it is hot but not boiling. Ask an adult to help you take the milk off the heat.

2. Add 4 tablespoons of vinegar.

3. Stir the mixture until it goes lumpy. Let it cool.

4. Pour the milk through a sieve to separate the lumps from the liquid. The lumps are your plastic! It is a polymer called casein.

5. Make sure it is cool, and then knead it in your hands. It will become like modelling clay.

New plastics

Carothers' team made several useful plastics. The first was neoprene, which is artificial rubber. Next, the team found that some plastics could be spun and stretched to make fibres. They decided to try and make a plastic that was like silk. They made and tested 81 different plastics, looking for one with the right **properties**. It took more than a year to make and test all these different polymers.

Eventually, in 1934, they created a plastic that could be spun into silky fibres. In 1935 DuPont named it nylon and **patented** it. Nylon was first used to make stockings. Today, it is used to make jackets, bags, tents, carpets, and ropes, as well as many other things.

The toughest plastic

Another important plastic was discovered at DuPont in 1965. Research chemist Stephanie Kwolek found a polymer that did not melt. It formed a cloudy liquid instead. The technicians refused to try and spin this new material. They said it would block up the machine, but Kwolek persuaded them to try.

Bioplastic

Most plastics do not rot, so rubbish dumps are full of plastic waste that will be there for hundreds of years. One invention that is helping to reduce this problem is bioplastic, made from starch. Starch is a natural polymer found in plants. It will rot in soil or on a compost heap instead of adding to a rubbish mountain. Bioplastic is very useful for things that don't need to last a long time, such as plastic bags.

The new material did not block the spinning machine, however. The thread it produced was incredible! It was five times stronger than steel, and it was extremely stiff. The new material was named Kevlar. Kevlar is used today for bullet-proof clothing and in car parts and some tyres. It is also part of many **composites**, or combined materials.

Kevlar is bullet-proof, so it is used to make soldiers' helmets. It is also used in bicycle frames and tennis rackets.

Composites

<u>A composite is a combination of two materials that make a new material with improved qualities.</u> One material is usually strong but brittle material, such as glass fibre. This is mixed with another material that is tough and does not snap or break easily. The result is a very strong, lightweight material. Composites are used in high-performance cars, aircraft, spacecraft, and sports equipment. Some aircraft, such as this B-2 bomber, have an outer skin made of composites. The material absorbs **radar** waves and makes the B-2 "invisible" to radar.

Miracle Medicines

Chemistry has been important in the invention of medicines. For thousands of years, humans have used natural substances to help heal wounds and cure illness. But as scientific investigation has progressed, new medicines have been invented, and they have saved millions of lives.

Antibiotics

Microbes are microscopic forms of life. **Bacteria** are types of microbes, and some bacteria get in people's bodies and make them ill. Antibiotics are used as medicine to stop infections caused by bacteria and other microbes. The first antibiotics were found by investigating many different chemicals.

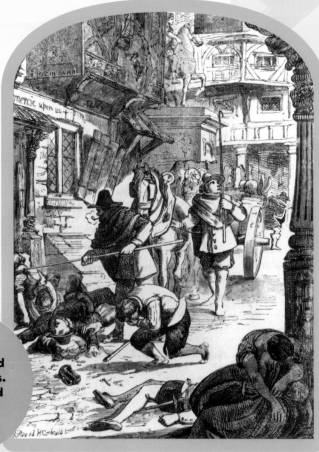

In the days before antibiotics, diseases such as bubonic plague would sweep through cities, killing thousands. This print shows the collection of dead bodies during the Great Plague of London in 1665.

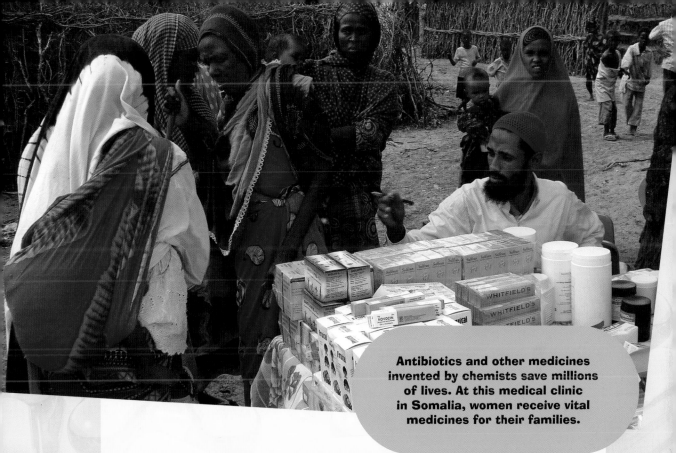

Antibiotics and other medicines invented by chemists save millions of lives. At this medical clinic in Somalia, women receive vital medicines for their families.

Gerhard Domagk was a German **chemist** at a dye company called IG Farben. Domagk decided to test IG Farben's dyes to see if any of them had a medical use. He was looking particularly for a medicine that could kill bacteria, because bacteria cause most diseases. In 1932, Domagk found that one dye, Prontosil, stopped wounds from getting infected. It also cured many diseases caused by bacteria.

How did it work?

Many scientists began studying Prontosil. They were trying to understand why it was successful. They found that one part of the Prontosil **molecule** affected the bacteria's growth.

Once they understood how Prontosil worked, chemists were able to make similar medicines that worked better. Prontosil and related medicines cured many people before they were replaced by even better medicines, such as penicillin.

Targeting pathogens

Biochemistry is the study of the thousands of chemical reactions that happen in living things. A chemical reaction happens when one substance reacts with another and changes. A **chemical pathway** is a sequence of chemical reactions in living **cells**.

In the 1950s, US biochemists Gertrude Elion and George H. Hitchens developed a new approach to finding medicines. Earlier researchers had tested chemicals, looking for ones that affected **pathogens**. Pathogens are microbes that cause disease. Elion and Hitchens started by studying the pathogens instead. What chemical pathways did the microbes have that were not found in humans? When they found a difference, they tried to make medicines that could affect that chemical pathway. They were able to create medicines that killed pathogens but did not hurt humans.

New medicines are often tested on animals before they are tested on human beings. Some people object to such animal testing.

Successful new drugs

Elion and Hitchens invented many new medicines using their method. They found the first medicine to help people with leukaemia (cancer of the blood). They also found the first medicine that acted against viruses, which are tiny microbes that destroy living cells. Elion and Hitchings also invented the first medicines that stopped human bodies from rejecting new organs. This helped patients to survive operations such as heart or kidney transplants.

A new way to deliver medicine has recently been invented. The medicine is attached to tiny **particles** known as nanoparticles. The striped nanoparticles shown here can carry medicine right inside a cell.

The placebo effect

Sometimes, just believing that a medicine will work helps people get better. This is known as the **placebo** effect. It can be used when testing to see if new medicines really work. The patients being tested are divided into two groups. One group is given the medicine, and the other group takes a placebo – something that looks the same but contains no medicine. The results are compared.

Imagine you had just invented a new medicine. What if the placebo group improved as much as the people who got the real medicine? Would you believe your new medicine really worked? Or would you want to do some more investigating?

EXPLORING THE UNIVERSE

For thousands of years, people looked at the night sky and wondered about the stars. What are they? Why do they seem to move across the sky? They had no real answers to these questions. <u>In the last few hundred years, however, new inventions have increased our knowledge of the universe</u>.

Ancient astronomers

Astronomers are scientists who study the planets and space. More than 2,000 years ago, Chinese and Indian astronomers were studying the night skies. These ancient astronomers discovered a lot about the movement of the Sun, Moon, and stars simply by watching the sky and keeping careful records.

Astronomers study the night skies in places called observatories. This observatory, Jantar Mantar in Jaipur, India, was built in the early 17th century.

Between the 10th and 16th centuries, astronomers in India, China, and the Middle East began to use observatories – places to observe, or look at, the night sky. They made giant instruments designed to measure the Sun, Moon, and stars.

Telescopes

In 1608, a Dutch maker of glasses, Hans Lippershey, created one of the first telescopes. The great Italian scientist Galileo first used the telescope for astronomy. He built a telescope that magnified 20 times. He turned it on the night skies and quickly made several discoveries. For example, he was the first to discover that the planet Jupiter had moons circling round it.

An astronaut repairs the powerful Hubble Space Telescope, which sends images of the distant universe back to Earth.

New knowledge

As scientists carry out new investigations and make new discoveries, it can change our view of the world – or of the whole universe! In ancient times, humans believed that Earth was the centre of the universe. However, astronomers overturned this idea. They showed that Earth and other planets orbit (go round) the Sun. This idea was first suggested by the ancient Greek astronomer Aristarchus in 260 BC. In 1543, the Polish astronomer Nicolaus Copernicus showed this was true.

Rocket science

The telescope expanded our knowledge of space, but it could not help us to get there. For that, we needed a rocket.

US scientist Robert H. Goddard was the first person to build a modern rocket. He launched his rocket in 1926. The experimental rockets built by Goddard in the 1930s led to more powerful rockets in the 1940s and 1950s. In Germany in 1942, the first rocket ever to reach space was launched. In 1957, Russian scientists launched a rocket that carried the first **satellite** into space to orbit Earth.

Twelve years later, in 1969, the first people landed on the Moon. So in a period of less than 70 years, inventors took us from thinking about rockets to walking on the Moon!

Expanding universe

Inventions such as telescopes and rockets have completely changed our view of the universe. In Galileo's time, even the most advanced scientists thought that the solar system was the whole universe. Today, we know that the Sun is just one star in the Milky Way – a huge **galaxy** containing billions of stars! And beyond the Milky Way are billions of other galaxies.

The Space Shuttle is launched by a rocket but returns to Earth like an aeroplane.

Space inventions

Space exploration has produced all kinds of inventions that we use right here on Earth.

- Joysticks used for computer games were invented for the Lunar Rover, a vehicle that astronauts used to get around on the Moon.

- Pens that work when held upside down were used in spaceships, where there isn't enough gravity to make ink flow downwards.

- Transparent teeth braces are made from a tough material developed for spacecraft.

- TV satellite dishes use technology invented for satellites.

- Firefighters' suits and ski boots both use materials first invented for spacesuits.

- Smoke detectors in your home are based on a detector invented for a space station.

- Cordless tools were developed so that astronauts could drill for rock samples on the Moon.

- Trainer insoles use "viscoelastic" bubbles copied from a material invented to cushion astronauts during blast-off.

Astronauts used the newly invented joystick to control the Lunar Rover on the Moon.

Inventions Timeline

This timeline shows just a few of the many thousands of inventions that took place in the last 400 years.

1608	Hans Lippershey makes one of the first telescopes.
1657	Christiaan Huygens invents the first pendulum clock.
1712	Thomas Newcomen makes the first successful steam engine design.
1780	William Addis makes some of the first toothbrushes.
1831	Michael Faraday demonstrates his first electric **generator**.
1839	Charles Goodyear invents a process to make weatherproof rubber.
1878–1880	Thomas Alva Edison and Joseph Swan make usable light bulbs.
1887–1888	Nikola Tesla invents an AC motor.
1904	John Fleming makes a **vacuum** tube.
1926	Robert Goddard launches the first practical liquid-fuelled rocket.
1932	Gerhard Domagk makes the antibiotic Prontosil.
1934	Wallace Carothers makes nylon.
1946	ENIAC, the first programmable, general-purpose electronic computer, is made. Percy L. Spencer invents the microwave oven.
1958–1959	Jack S. Kilby and Robert Noyce produce the first **microchips**.
1965	Stephanie Kwolek makes Kevlar.
1969	The first part of the Internet is put together.
1990	Tim Berners-Lee invents the World Wide Web.
2005	Michael Bowers makes a white LED light.
2007	A **nanotube** radio is made at the Lawrence Berkeley National Laboratory in the USA.

Glossary

amplifier device that amplifies, or makes radio signals stronger

bacteria microscopic, single-celled life forms

battery device that stores electrical energy

breakthrough sudden successful development, such as an invention or advance in knowledge

cell very small piece of living matter that is the basic unit in all living things. Some life forms have just one cell. The human body has trillions of cells.

chemical pathway sequence of chemical reactions in living cells, such as the cells in your body

chemist scientist who works in the area of chemistry, which is the study of substances and their properties

circuit arrangement of parts through which an electric current can flow

composite combination of two materials to make a new material with improved qualities

crystal solid that forms in a regular pattern, like a diamond

current stream or flow, such as an electrical current, which is a stream of electricity

diode device that controls the flow of an electric current

dynamo type of generator that produces direct-current (DC) electricity

efficient producing results with little waste of energy

electrode wire used as a conductor of electricity

electronic having to do with electric devices such as televisions and computers that are developed using electronics. Electronics is a science that studies and uses the flow of electricity.

emission substance released into the air, such as gases released by the burning of petroleum and other fossil fuels

engineer scientist who works in the area of engineering, which includes the study and use of machines and structures

filament wire in a light bulb that glows and gives off light

galaxy group of stars, solar systems, gases, and matter within the universe

generator machine that produces electrical energy from kinetic (movement) energy

inefficient wasteful of energy or not able to work well

mains electricity electricity supplied by a central power station

microbe microscopic form of life

microchip tiny electrical circuit that contains many transistors and other parts

molecule group of atoms joined together

nanotube extremely tiny tubes that are 10,000 times finer than a human hair

particle small piece of matter

patent right given to an inventor to be the only person to make or sell an invention for a certain period of time

pathogen microbe that causes disease

placebo something that looks like a medicine but contains no healing powers. Placebos are used to test if newly invented medicines really work.

pollutant something that causes pollution, or makes air, water, or land dirty

polymer large molecule made up of a chain of smaller molecules

property quality of a substance, such as strength, sweetness, or ability to conduct electricity

radar device that detects objects or movement by picking up radio waves

radio wave type of electromagnetic wave that is used for radio, television, and radar communication. An electromagnetic wave is a wave of energy moving through space. Light and X-rays are other types of electromagnetic waves.

satellite object that travels in a circle around another object. Also, human-made objects sent into space to orbit Earth

theory idea that explains why or how something happens. If theories in science are tested and proven many times, they become accepted as facts.

valve device that can be opened and closed to control the flow of something, such as electricity or fluid

vacuum condition or space created when all or most of the air has been removed from a space or container

Find out more

Books

Dead Famous: Inventors and Their Mad Ideas, Mike Goldsmith (Scholastic Hippo, 2002)

Eyewitness: Invention, Lionel Bender (Dorling Kindersley, 2005)

A Painful History of Medicine: Pills, Powders and Potions, John Townsend (Raintree, 2006)

Reinvent the Wheel: Make Classic Inventions, Discover Your Problem-solving Genius and Take the Inventor's Challenge, Ruth Kassinger (Jossey Bass, 2001)

A Weird History of Science: Outrageous Inventions, John Townsend (Raintree, 2006)

Websites

www.pbs.org/tesla/ins/
Tesla: Master of Lightning: Inside the Lab
Learn about the AC generator, the AC motor, and some of Tesla's other inventions.

www.bbc.co.uk/history/british/victorians/launch_ani_beam_engine.shtml
The Beam Engine Animation
Build your own steam engine.

www.greatachievements.org
Greatest Engineering Achievements of the 20th Century
Investigate great engineering inventions, such as the aeroplane and the computer.

www. smith.edu/hsc/museum/ancient_inventions/hsclist.htm
Smith College Museum of Ancient Inventions
Look at some really old inventions, such as eyeliner and catapults!

Research a great invention

Penicillin has been one of the most useful antibiotics of all, but it was discovered by accident. Who discovered it, and how?

The two people who made the first successful powered aeroplane spent many years investigating and developing ideas before they finally succeeded. Can you find out more about their story?

Do you remember ENIAC on page 21? It was only one of several early computers. Can you find out about others, such as the Colossus and the Z3?

Index